The Book of Rosiah

By

Johnathan Abraham Antelept

Table of Contents

I. HERALD

Mysterious Origins

From whence did he come?
Why is favor shown upon him?
When it's all said and done,
All the trial was favor…

As the mission kept its call
Ever-pressing, ever-present.
At the source of the seed
Bears the fruit of dedication,
At the root unto all.

Born on the plains,
His mother was waning,
Complications from labor…
Running from strictures
Her heart had grown warmer,
Yet the risk was much greater.
Roaming the land in search for a freedom…

She nestled him close to her bosom and knew,
As told by the visions, the feeling transmitted.
Not quite knowing why each action was needed,
Yet guided by sentience of higher ordering warble…

Blooming with blue,
Everesce was her name,
Ice crystals forming on lips of fragility.
A pulse that was wavering like American hegemony,
A new era was emerging from her womb…they shall see…
She died in the midday sun of deep autumn.

Everesce, at home in the whistling wind,
In the forests and the streams of Ancient Man's Dreams.
Freed from obstruction to herald the highlands,
A cooling splash dousing the countryside wondrous.

Unsure, the populace all felt it within,
Yet obscure and somewhat distant from them,
They kept it hidden and for many it passed by without awareness…

Two days and nights,
Wrapped in the cloth of its milky supreme,
Of the stars that dripped eons more ancient than Earth.
He suckled its breast,
But the wind parched his lips,
While vultures took heed and hovered with hunger.
His eyes wide like gates opened everlasting confession…
From before the birth of light to beyond the end of time.

Farmer John and his dog came passing in route.
Standing before him, slackened, entranced…
The baby with eyes like an owl,
Orbs of black wellspring, twinkling inklings of otherness…
Of brotherhood, of sisterhood, of marvel and majesty,
Like standing before his father just born…
An eerie sense of forefather younger.

John carried the baby to his house for some water,
Golden sashes bristling in the briskness of November.

Upon returning to the field his mother no more,
No trace or indentation in grasses…
The sweet smell of lilac arousing an awe.

A Message from Enoch

That night John dreamt of a vision.
There appeared a glowing emerald
Set in a golden diadem
Off in the distance where all else was dark…
Then it vanished…

From forth there was a shimmering,
In a robe of scarlet red,
A hooded figure named Enoch…
His face could not be seen.

He spoke with a heavy tongue,
Of an Ancient Melody,
While he held Rosiah tenderly…

"There is a King that has come from underground,
That will rise to the peak…
Where the pyramid will be placed on his back upside down,
The foundation for generations to come…
Rosiah Rose Rephaiah."

In the arms of Enoch, Rosiah was handed to John.

II. ODYSSEY

On the Plains

John taught Rosiah how to fish, to build, to hunt and to farm.
He taught him how to fight and how to be fair,
But more importantly, how to love and how to make peace.
He fed him with heartiness and loved him with wonder,
But never told him of the vision he had,
Nor of the mystery of his mother.

Rosiah sensed silence impregnated with truth.
Silence he tried to pierce, but could not rip the bubble.
He suspected he came from afar,
But more so he felt an immensity within.
His hunger was deeper than John's wisdom…

In the 15th year of Rosiah,
John was approaching his death.
Lying weak in his bed nearly left from the pain,
He told Rosiah he was King,
But had no time to say more.
Rosiah stood over his head, with eyes like an owl,
Humming the songs he had sung since he was young,
Songs which John had never taught him.
The songs carried John's spirit away…
Rosiah drifted deeper in wildness of heart.

John had no family besides Rosiah,
So after his passing Rosiah took responsibility of the farm.
He planted wheat, tended chickens and goats by the pasture.
He fished to let his mind settle and ease,
His confusion arousing his anger,
Of some knowledge beneath a shroud which was calling,
A knowledge which underlay all.

Soon thereafter, a hunger to know compelled him to go.
He felt in his heart that the sun would not set
If he kept in motion towards the West and beyond.
Maybe motion and time would bring truth.

Rosiah Roams Westbound

He spent years on the road singing songs.
On the corners of small towns he would lay his hat down,
Then vanish just as quickly as the wind he rode in on,
Following his spirit.
He travelled down the coast and saw the cities in sprawl,
And sat his hat down just the same.

For years he fled, from city to city,
Eating scraps that they tossed him to appease,
For his money grew thin much too quick;
Working odd jobs fixing drains,
Repairing porches and changing tires…
Walking barefoot at times just to breathe.
Relieving the strictures they placed abound,
Like Everesce, he wanted to be free.

He had a woman or two lay inside of his bag for a night
With the heat combining in swirl…
He dreamt that he'd find an Ancient Poetess
To share his songs with,
And bare his heart to by the fires.
He looked in their eyes,
But the horizons kept calling his gaze.
His eyes like an owl, piercing like flame,
Burning with a hunger for ultimate wisdom,
As if he were destined to seek it.

Mexico and the Desert

Rosiah grew tired of cities,
And the consumption abound.
He set his sight south towards the desert.

His eyes became hawk-like, more hungry and slender,
With the whipping wind making his vision only clearer.
To the interiors of Mexico he travelled by foot.
To the interiors of his being he sought.

For years he wandered through the desert.

His confusion was the reason, commanding his attention,
Putting him plush against self.
He examined his corridors, his dreams and desires.
He cast off influence from all he had known.
He looked for *The Source* in silence and scorching sun.
He waited for moons and seraphs to invite him
Up higher to give him a view.
All the while Rosiah sang and his songs only deepened,
Like a hawk in the day and an owl through the night.

Settling into the Forest

Slowly he journeyed in deep.
He made his way south to the tropics.
The forests arose with magnitude and magnanimity, of flora and fauna.
The stark contrast put oil upon his lips.
He entered the forest with wet ears.

Night after night, he bore the night…
His eyes like an owl…aware of what lurked.
Predators were entranced by the scent of his flesh,
Yet repelled by something that aired through their marrow…

Through time Rosiah approached them.
He made friends with the panther and befriended the jaguar,
And gained respect of the puma just by locking its eye.
Their lust for his flesh turned into love.

The forest seemed endless in scope.
For a while he thought this was so,
And found a home in the roughage of fecundity,
And richness of dankness.

Rosiah oozed with the sweat of immersion and lust.
He was musky with the fermentation of his songs.
His voice grew husky in the humidity of the plushness,
The rush of the jump from the waterfall to river,
The swimming cacophony of amphibians
And brightly plumed toucans weaving through branches,
The wind wafting romantics, whispering secrets,
Telling of hillscapes with bounteous foliage…

Rosiah remembered the terraces, the terminals,
The shining night lights and amenities,
But he thought of expenditures and the adventures were contrived,
Always with a dollar sign nestled thereunder.
He remembered the cityscape…never settled,
Always restless unless engorged with some other affliction.
There were prices to pay for 'freedom.'

Rosiah made woodwork and even a flute
In the dank ambiance of the forest.
For hours he enriched the trees and the fauna
With otherworldly dreams he was instilled with from birth.

Every now and then, he remembered his beginnings with his father,
And remembered the diligence and stalwart regard,
The clear-eyed focus and attention,
And the fairness he laid down on the fields that came before him.

Again he felt the sting of not knowing where he came from,
Not quite knowing where he stood,
And rather for the matter, unclear as to exactly where he was going.
Society had told him what to say and how to be,
What options there were for what to do…
Though this was not enough for Rosiah to rise
Into true awareness of all that surrounded him,
And to root himself to the source deep inside of him.

Love and Lust

One day Rosiah lay on a ridge
By the waterfall
Flowing into a basin…

There appeared in the basin a woman
With ripped cargo pants and a backpack.
She was dripping wet with sweat…
He felt love for her instantly.

She put down her pack and took out some soap,
Then undressed herself slowly…

Entering the water, she began to bathe,
And Rosiah could not look away…

She was almond eyed,
With almond colored thighs and black hair.
He fell entranced by her beauty,
And his heart swelled with song!

His flute began to sing of a hovering dove,
Floating and diving in oil and wine,
Softening the skin the softer…

Hearing his song, like honey on her ears,
And a presence that was prescient,
She was not afraid.

Rosiah emerged from the trees slowly,
Watching her watch him,
Watching her wondrously…

And her eyes were pools of raspberry rose,
Drowning and rising.
And her heart was mango melting,
Watching Rosiah.

Her eyes were like marshmallows melting before…
Rosiah Rose Rephaiah.

Passion and Pain

Many days and weeks passed,
Maybe months or a year,
Time was the time between lovemaking
And the time of the love they expressed went on well,
For days and weeks,
Maybe months or a year,
The swelling and throbbing of attachment.

But as things progressed, the woman began to wonder,
What it was to be loved by someone else.
She wondered if her beauty could inspire even more.

She wondered what other men might do,
What wealth it would bring,
What power it would hold in the cities.
Could it be the key to her dreams?

Rosiah sensed a tenuousness…
But just as soon as they loved,
He needed her skin, her soft moans, her warm touch once again.
Her eyes were filled with love, and her lotus bloomed for him,
She loved him, her heart overflowed.
Still, *love was just not enough*.

One day Rosiah awakened to find the woman gone.
He turned toward, inward with shock and dismay.
His heart then felt caved and crumbling stone…
Like the sweets on the tooth,
So sweet when she left there was holes.

Rosiah went on and still sang a deep song,
But it wasn't as before.
The forest he had called home was not calming to him.
The home he had known wasn't there.

And the love he had known made it bare,
Removing the aura of rubbing on stones
For hours, skin pressed against skin.
Her flower made nectar that would drip down his mane
Staining his memories with addiction.

Rosiah felt again, a confusion, interrupted,
His clarity removed by the absence of her,
But weeks turned into months and months into years,
As he wandered the addiction grew dim and he wondered…

He wondered what lie on the edge of the forest,
If he kept moving away from where he had begun in the fields,
In the pastures of wheat yellow bronze in the sun,
Father John in the wind looking over.

Out of the Forest, Southbound

Rosiah rose and took straight to the South,
To the mouth of the beast which many tried to run from;
The yawning unknown where his dreams cast adumbrations from.
Something kept calling, cajoling and crying.
A hunger he'd known now resurfaced more forceful.

He saw on the edge of the forest, the dozers,
Steadily encroaching upon the nests
And leveling ponds to compress an ounce of gravel
Into profits much less than which stood in nature
With more silver and splendor.

As he walked through construction sites
He saw the workers sweating
And directing operations with weary concern.
As Rosiah stood watching,
His soul felt a pang at the sight of them burning in plight.
They worked unbeknownst to the stillness of his stance,
His eyes like an owl, absorbing their burning.

He kept moving south
Through cities and villages singing his songs,
Playing mellifluous, melodious flute for a meal,
Shaking hands, looking long in their eyes,
Loving that moment…
Yet always watching it fleeting
Like butterflies dancing in winds
Of some impending engagement
Or fear of a stranger's presence.
With eyes of black wellspring
He drunk of it well.

One day in travelling south…
Something came bellowing;
A sharp like contusion hit him below,
His eyes opened evermore…
Stopping on a dime
Like father time whispering some soliloquy more ancient than tongue.
Knowing he must move east towards the rising sun,

For the dawn of a new day and New Era!

Eastbound, Towards the Rising Sun

Rosiah walked for weeks,
Singing songs where he could to get sustenance
Or money for some food,
More intensity in his eyes,
More hungry for what was calling.
Making it to the shore, he saw it stretched endless in both directions,
And the sea spanned infinite.
He stood for a while and reflected…

Something was drawing his soul into the sea…

He sat down and looked out towards the sea,
Trying to pierce through to the end of eternity.
For hours he sat and looked on.
He came from so far,
For so long he had travelled…
Feeling dejected he fell asleep on the beach
As the waves rolled and receded with ease.

Soon the night swelled upon,
And the winds picked up.
The rains began to pound,
But Rosiah found it enlivening, awaking and rising,
Standing amidst the sirens of the lightning.
He cackled and howled in unison with the storm.
It kept his mind clear from a tearing confusion.

Through the lightning blanching the grey sky swirling,
Rosiah apprehended a mountain way off in the distance,
An island of a mountain.

The splendor of it took him and poured in trepidation.
It rose from the depths of the ocean,
Piercing past clouds jutting space.
Standing, residing…presiding.

It called his name repeatedly.

It explained to him of greatness.
It chastised his fear and awed him to tears.
In his dreams it spoke to him and told him:

The Word of the Summit

"Only the King of Kings could understand the vista my summit gleams! Only the most diligent could weather such a trek! Only the hungriest to see would succeed. I stand here for a reason, and my reason is often feared. I am placed outside of boxes, on horizons unimagined, my air so rarefied that the breath cannot sustain, only if the air is rising out of you which gives life."

"Demons have tried to conquer my heights, but found lost in themselves as they tried. Adventurers have risen to the challenge to accomplish, but ceased to remain stalwart when they realized what they saw. They receded when understood no one would greet them with applause, and the jaws of life were dormant, trembling on their heads, waiting for another meter or more to awaken....Wizards looked for incantations in the crust of my ridges, but found it was a code that couldn't be cracked. I've stood here for ages never swaying from men, only watching them meander around me. Watching them watch me and believe it wasn't real, that the path to rapture lay in what could be explained."

Crossing the Sea

Awakened like stranded seaweed,
Sea wreck from the sea,
His spirit began to bleed a fire to reach it…
Rosiah desired to see what the mountain peak spoke of…
And if he died in the climb he wished…
"May another man find inspiration in my corpse for ascension."
He rose.

Rosiah swam east toward the rising sun's glow,
In the mellowing waves flowing and throwing his soul,
In a motion of circular emotion, feeding his hunger.
His pace never wavered.
It was pure.

Through the sea he swam for the day,
And night came upon him,
Still he was miles and miles from the mountain.
Thousands of feet the water swooped deep,
And miles, stretching miles all around him.
This made Rosiah smile with confoundment.

Like a fountain that flows from the source and back into,
The waves fed him strength and his strength replenished them.
Rosiah's mind began to swivel on the hinge of a speck,
Opening doors through the ozone and beyond.
He felt a sense of knowing come upon...

For days Rosiah swam, with no water or lamb,
No supper or ale, for fortitude or strength.
He moved and was fed through the food that he fed to the sea;
The Stasis of Ultimicity...
The surrender to a power immeasurably much greater than his limbs
Could much muster,
So his limbs became the other,
And in the other there flowed all immensity through his limbs.
Rosiah could swim for a century or two.

For weeks Rosiah kept pace in this mystical stasis
And approached the mammoth of a mountain.
Its craggy shores were not sweet to the sores on his feet
Which were ripe from exposure.
Blood trickled down into the sea...

At the Base of the Summit

Rosiah breathed deep and took hold of a fish,
Removing the spine with the flick of his wrist,
Watching it wriggle and understanding its pain,
Suckling the flesh of even the eyeballs.

He looked up the monster which arose above clouds,
His eyes in amazement.
The mountain chuckled a bellow
At something he was yet to grasp and maybe never ever...

Rosiah responded with song, and the mountain listened,
Smitten in wondrous extension of apprehending,
Extending since the time it was created in stars,
When the iron was forged in explosions.

Rosiah had found that passion relieved his pain and confusion,
Resolving to climb the horizon to see over the cliff…
Diving without knowing into the unknown,
Not knowing what lies waiting in the abyss.
Still his hunger had led him to an unexpected absence…

Stranded on the mountain's craggy shore, he could only climb higher.
He could not go back for he knew not how to desire,
The shores and the fields where he left long ago.

Each time the confusion rose within him exorbitant,
He thrashed and writhed to subside it.
He was that lone pilot
Flying madly into the center of the iris of the swirling conundrum…
As the winds rushed around it increasingly quick,
The jangled and jiggled rhythmically rickety airliner,
Rushing into the center just to see what was there.
It was absence, so bare and confounding.

But this mountain presented a vision unimagined,
Unimaginably grander in scope than could be fathomed.
He began to drip and ooze with awe more fervent than ever,
That the highest heights may unfetter the feeling of confusion
Which enveloped the soul of his skeleton.
Leviathan was writhing in front and he wanted to wrestle,
Even if it meant he'd be torn by the muscle,
That immensity that suffused through his mind…
"Douse the mind in lava drinks and mold the mountain while it glows!"
Rosiah removed all his clothes and began the ascent
To the clime of the unknown,
Hopefully the most meaningful zone…

Making Music

His climb began jagged,
Piercing his hands and feet plenty,
The sweat stinging his eyes with frustration.
He cried and stammered to climb.
No matter!
Rosiah pushed forward and fierce,
Gouging the mountain to show it who'd come.
Rosiah punched a hole in its side as he lunged,
And beat the mountain like a drum.
He made music!

Singing his songs,
The songs only deepened to express what he was reaching to be.
Expanding, for what he was reaching to see was unplanned
And his steps were taken towards it
Even though he didn't understand it,
But he knew it was grander than grand and must be apprehended.

Ascending the Summit

Rosiah's beard grew.
Yearly it dangled lower,
Till he wrapped it around his own torso and loins.
His hands were like rock and his toes were like rock.
Rosiah Rose Rephaiah, the rock of the righteous!
He slept like a rock, and even ate rocks,
Grinding them to dust mixing with the rain and some seagulls.

For years he climbed harder.
The grey in his beard turned to snow,
And he wearied a little from the harshness of it all.
He began to doubt that he would understand
What he thought he could use to relieve his confusion, from it all.

III. KINGSHIP

The Eye of Yahweh

In the 80th year of Rosiah,
He sat on the edge of a ridge overlooking the expanses for days,
Still unable to apprehend the summit.
It seemed as if he would never reach it,
That his corpse would lie there and maybe another man would find it,
And use it as proof of his worth.

In the weeks thereafter,
In reflection and song, somber and sulking of how long he had writhed,
And how he still pushed,
But something which burned in his soul was flickering,
Fluttering, falling in forcefulness...

Yahweh watched close and had watched him for years,
Watching him climb and make music on the mountain.
The sky opened wide and it shone to the center of the Universal eye,
With purple and orange,
With white, grey and golden billowing pillows
Of clouds as lining to tunnel.
Yahweh gazed at him, iris to iris.

Rosiah peered looking into the eye for a lifetime, doubling his own.
Time took him in and swallowed him whole.
He lived for eighty more years,
Reflecting on the nature of existence,
Staring into the eye which just hummed.

When he snapped back he was filled with a wisdom beyond him.
His thoughts hummed much closer to the source of Earth's seed.
He gasped for breath and looked around him.
The sea stretched infinitely.
The mountain spanned downwards.
Though the depth of his mind stretched much deeper than the ocean,
The confusion at the bottom spanned deeper.

He blinked for a moment to feel his beard wrapped around him,
No longer white, but what it was like in youth.

The lines which he had felt on his face were now smooth.
When he blinked it was like the space between centuries.
Time had changed him and **Yahweh had saved him**.
His soul burned a slow inexorable fuel,
With an ozone glowing around him.

Rosiah sat cross-legged and soaked.
His hands touched the jagged rocks and they smoothed.
Love was like a wheel spinning endlessly up.
Rosiah sat and listened to everything for a week,
From across the seven seas,
From the alleyways and boroughs,
From the deserts, forests and rivers.
He could see past the ocean, past the land and beyond,
Until he saw his own self sitting there from abroad.
In that he smiled, and his smile turned to laughter,
A laughter which sprung from a well of depth deeper.
He simply opened his mouth and it flowed.

The Vista of the King of Kings

Rosiah looked upwards…
And saw the top of the mountain just a mile above him.
At the peak was a tree with purple fruit blooming.
Filled with awe at what he saw
He began to climb without rhyme or a reason…
Just the awe of the jaws of life yawning…

His wisdom was rich,
Yet it paled without fruit which called home such a vista.
The ice of crags sizzled his flesh,
So he wielded the flame of his own to address this,
His soul meshing well with anything oppressing.

The wind whipped and snapped him, pushing and pulling even more.
The clouds circled round, enveloping.
Lightning ripped right beside him and all around,
The thunder shaking his skeleton and loosening ligaments from fixings.
Still he climbed as if there were no sound,
Just a silent glowing, a pulsating peace, a flame of inexorable life.

Rosiah reached the top of the peak, with barely footing to stand.
The sky became luminous,
Shining a lustrous light.
He felt a love, he had never known approaching…

The Fruit of Persea, the Tree of Vitality and Destiny

Looking upon the tree
He sensed the roots sinking deeper than the mountain,
Into the ocean, to the bottom of sea,
Into the center of the Earth, deep entwined with her heart.

He kissed the base of her trunk with a tear.
The trunk was furry green, covered in moss,
And the fruit was swollen, ripe, looking like midnight purple pears.
Several dangled from branches with leaves of fresca blue.
The smell of the fruit overcame his elevation.

He picked a pear and held it.
It was heavy with juice.
It was thick and condensed.
It pumped and pulsed like a heart.
It beat like a heart!

He looked closer and examined its skin…
It was living.
The juice pulsed through its membranes…
It was living!

Rosiah placed his teeth on the edge of its skin.
It recoiled in reaction.
Watching it tremble, he could not devour.
Closing his eyes, he clutched it in tighter...
Taking a bite the juice rushed in flooding his mind
With a vortex of purpling, tunneling insight.
Through the eye of his *Father* he looked down below…
His head cocked back,
And his black eyes of orb turned golden with shimmering glow.
Tears of joy streamed his face with understanding.

Rosiah's confusion was gone…

Beholding the map of destiny,
From primeval time, to when time swore cease…
Allness, Nothingness and Simultaneity…
Infinite threads of the carpet enmeshed,
Turning in majestical fields of fresh herbs…
Lapis Lazuli descended on him.

From above came a bass, a hum which aligned:

"I am Yahweh…The Living One…eternally luminous. The Almighty, Most Gracious, Most Merciful. The One and only God. **I am the creator of all.** The storehouses of infinite bounty and vaults of ever-deepening wisdom reside in the timeless palace of my righteousness. All praise and worship is due unto I. All grace, wisdom and help is through me. In seeking wisdom…you have found me.

Rosiah, I have given you the Blueprint of Destiny and the Vista of Eternity. Go now and plant your seed in the soil of Earth. On every land and country your dreams shall manifest, but not every man will recognize your word…for your word is my word, and men have lost silence in cities and streets…Go now and carry forth my will from your loins."

IV. ZION

Preparations

Rosiah awoke on the shore of the beach that stretched endlessly far,
Feeling serene under eons abroad…
His eyes were golden wellsprings of wisdom,
Shining the truth of the Most High's decree.
His face was glowing resin,
Red like the wine from the richest vineyard vine.
His cloak was plush purple
And his head was bowed low,
Dripping with the oil of consecration.
The King of Judah, crowned and anointed.
Love in his heart,
Alight like a flame!

Rosiah began to build…
He made implements from small trees and stones.
He chopped logs for the structure,
And constructed a mast,
Patiently sewing the cloth to catch wind.

For 40 days and 40 nights Rosiah ate nothing,
But worked with little rest
To build a ship to sail east,
But first to head north,
And return to the land he had known…

Setting Sail

On the 41st day
Rosiah awoke and looked upon his ship.
It was stern and steady,
Stretching some 40 feet,
With a mast about 30 high.

He walked into the brush to pick mango and papaya.
Then sat beneath a Ceiba Tree…
Looking up through its branches,
He felt the love of Yahweh.

Rosiah savored the mango and papaya,
And his eyes felt an opening,
A resurgence from his fast.
He had paid food no mind
As he worked to build the ship
That would take him back to Ancient Origins,
And consequently a New Era.

He tossed the mango and papaya skin 'pon the ground
And strode through the vines,
Back towards the shore,
When a young Indigenous Man stepped forth,
And stood in his path.
His hair braided thick down his back,
The skin of a puma on his loins…
With eyes like a spear
The young man swore:

"My name is Nahual.
I know who you are and why you have come,
My people have been waiting for Salvation."

Rosiah said, "Come along…
There is respite and respect in me.
You shall be protected and loved, Nahual."

Nahual's eyes softened and tears came forth…
He fell to his face and thanked him.
They walked side by side to the shore,
Both pushing the ship into the sea.

Journeying Northbound

Rosiah fell into a trance,
Meditating on the pulse of the Galaxy's dance,
Kept in balance by the thread of the master weaver's mastery.

He saw patterns interlaced in patterns,
But his mind's eye remained clear crystal,
Just reflecting a rainbow on through.

On the island of Jamaica
Rosiah docked to gather papaya.
Not a city seemed close,
Nor a man could be seen.
Nahual lay asleep on the wooden deck darkening.
The sun was ripening fruit all the coast.

He found a tree replete with delectable juice…
So Rosiah divested his cloak
And threw papayas upon it,
To wrap them up well
And carry them back to the ship.

Kneeling down and assembling the fruit
He discovered a shadow overarching his work…
He looked up and saw a Rasta man watching,
His face was with a serene smile, as if knowing.
Dreadlocks flowing,
Down to the soil…
His hands were strong
From tilling the land.

The Rasta said deep,
"If it was Selassie that came for us…
Who is Rosiah?
For centuries we have walked in scorn and injustice.
For centuries we have longed to return to the root.
And now my eyes widen with the presence of truth.
Praise Jah of his coming!
At your service my King…by my soul I pledge Zion!"
Then the Rasta man bowed down
And tears fell from his cheeks,
For he knew his people were to be freed from Babylon's lies.

Rosiah looked upon him with compassion and love,
Kneeling down he placed his arm around his shoulder…
He said, "Come with me,
You shall have recognition…
Your humanity shall be honored,
Justice shall be metered,

And peace will be upon you.
All that you've done for Yah has been noticed."

The Rasta man ran to get a large net he used to fish with,
And helped Rosiah fill it with papaya.
They took it back to the ship,
Whereupon, Rosiah said to Rasta…"Nahual is your brother."
And to Nahual Rosiah said:
"Rasta is the same…brotherhood shall reign."
Nahual and Rasta looked upon each other with love.
Thereby they set sail Northbound once again.

The United States of America

Rosiah, Nahual and Rasta approached Virginia.
There they docked to find bread from a vendor.
Walking through the wealth and businesses,
They passed into the part of town where few people venture…

The factories were desolate
And the homes were shanty.
The streets were rough and cracked.
Stray dogs chewed on scraps,
Stray cats walked through alleys…

Rosiah saw a lone vendor
With a cart full of loaves
Wrapped in separate plastic bags,
In front of a business boarded up….

The vendor was an Appalachian man with a blonde shaggy beard,
His hands were rough and dirt was under his nails.
His eyes told tales of tough times…many stories…
He stood up from his stool as Rosiah approached,
His mouth gaping, and eyes like caverns.

The vendor said, "My name is Ericson, my Lord,
I had a vision of you, some years ago…
I was working in the mines
When a beam fell on my leg
And broke it severely…

They could not get to me for hours,
I lied scared in the dark,
Thinking my last moments were near.
Your face appeared at my most helpless moment.
I felt comforted when I saw you.
I had never forgotten that vision.
Take this bread at no charge, my Lord."

Then he bowed down, overcome, and cried in joy.
Rosiah welled with tears and looked upon him with love,
He touched him on his shoulder and said:

"Though you found more home in this place
Than Nahual and Rasta,
You were overlooked and exploited
By the same men who waxed poetic on 'freedom.'
Come with me and you shall find truth and healing."
Then he turned to all three of them and said:

"No matter the hue, no matter the custom, the same force of life is a
gift from my *Father*...Do the will of Yahweh by loving your brother."

Nahual, Rasta and Ericson united.

The four of them came back to the ship
And set sail Northbound once again.
Rosiah was headed towards the epicenter of 'The System.'
His eyes lit like torches in the night,
Guiding the way to salvation...

Washington D.C.

Rosiah's ship docked several miles south of D.C.
Nahual, Rasta and Ericson followed Rosiah as he walked,
Through the streets, by the businesses and beyond.

Rosiah's pace was steady and swift.
His eyes were piercing flame...

Soon they came to the Washington Monument and stood.
Rosiah closed his eyes and took a deep breath...

Like the swell from the ocean,
Like the rush over rivers,
Like the wish over forests,
And the wash over mountains,
And the whip over desert like stone…

Then he raised his hands and head to Yahweh.

"Bringeth the harbinger to herald the harbinger,
O Holy One Supreme!"

The sky opened up and a green light descended upon Rosiah.
The city stood still, in a trance when it came.
A horn pierced the city, shaking buildings,
Disrupting meetings, bringing planes into emergency landings.
The horn pierced the sky 7 times.
Nahual, Rasta and Ericson ran out of fear,
They hid in the bushes
And watched Rosiah levitate in the Light of the One.

People from across the city gathered round Rosiah.
The president and his retinue came from behind them.
Transfixed, the people paid no attention to the president…

The Word Against Babylon

Rosiah looked upon the people,
Young…Old…
Rich…Poor…
Men…Women…
Of all complexions…
Each of them looking upon Rosiah, transfixed.

Rosiah spoke to them thus:

"Have we not turned and tossed in sleep too long? Have we not toiled
the skin raw down to the bone? Have we not had our fill of the
murders, of the theft, of the double speaking contrivance that makes
the Word dull?

Why have you committed to *poison*?...The seas fill with toxins. The air thickens with fumes. The soil collects runoff and you water your fields with tint. Still you proclaim this is advancement...To perish by the ingenuity of your own hand? Still you worship the works of your own hands more than Yah. If you only chose life...

What compelled you to build bridges across canyons, skyscrapers taller than mountains and spacecrafts sent to space? Yet the homeless man beseeches for some change to get a sandwich and you sneer your face and look down upon him. The single mother struggles with no father for son's guidance, so you blame the little one because he sought guidance from a sick society. The widow descends into the depths of loneliness with millions crowded close, aloof in their strivings.

Why has the African been attacked and defamed when he birthed you?...Gifted you the knowledge which you honor as your own...but you took it, twisted it and misunderstood its essential application...

Why have the Indigenous peoples of the Earth become destitute while your cities condense with gems, steel and gold? Your wealth is a stolen wealth! Your museums are rife with the conquest of merchants thieving from tombs to profit their palaces! And your schools tell the lies of the oppressor...

Why have you lost sight of the Earth which encompasses you? You disrespect the land with your feverish greed. Why have you reduced life to a squabbling over scraps? No matter how much you amass you cannot take it to that which is after. Now if you only chose life, you would have richness everlasting...

Your institutions are dry and cold, callous, nay...even abusive. Your churches are confused and lost, far away from the root. Your synagogues are full of the faithless, deluded as if they were chosen by Yah...Only spirit and truth will suffice!

Oh Babylon! You've deceived many, but I see your true face! Academia knows no Wisdom! The hospitals know no healing! Government knows not democracy! And the corporations ravage with gluttony! *All wisdom, healing and power is of Yah!*

Why have you lifted up a *piece of paper* above Yahweh? You've deified that which is death! Your spirits lie dormant, so your pain is a birth pang! Your pain is destruction! The birth of Zion is close at hand!

From our Ancient Root there is life…From our Ancient Origin we shall blossom again.

Zion is close at hand!"

After uttering these words
The people grew restless,
A resistance of a mob began,
Shouts of "Liar!" and "Racism!" were heard,
Some said to "Grab him!"…"Kill him!"

The sky opened up and Rosiah was lifted by a green light.
A horn pierced the city,
7 times it resounded.
The people became frightened,
Some falling to their face with their hands overhead,
While others ran away screaming…

The secret service rushed the president back to his car,
And took off through the city
Blowing its horn wildly
With police escorts sirening
Cutting through traffic.

Rasta man smiled and looked at Nahual and Ericson and said:
"I know where he's going."

Ancient Origins, Zion, A New Earth

Rosiah opened his eyes and knelt in his ship…
Seeing down miles the lights in a whirl,
Hearing the sirens and alarms in a swirl.

Rosiah, serene, undocked his ship,
And prayed to Yahweh for a slipstream effect,

Falling in perfect accord it was carried 'cross the sea...
For weeks eating dried papaya...
Finally approaching the Strait of Gibraltar.
The memory of the Moors was ripe on the water.

Through the Mediterranean Sea
He entered the Nile
On a swift slipstream...
Effortlessly moving upstream,
Through Lower Egypt
Up through the Valley of Kings,
Where Rosiah was ascended,
And Lazuli was his.

Through Nubia passing,
The Nile was rich,
And Rosiah relived
The depth of Man's history,
The deeper he went
The root came closer...

The Nile River valley,
Flooding with insight and innovation,
Where Punt was the ancestral homeland of Kemet,
As attested by the Egyptians themselves...
The root of a ripening vine.

See the White Nile and Nile was Gihon,
And the Blue Nile was Pishon,
From the Garden of Eden, with Adam and Eve...

Eden...our origin...
The birthplace of man,
From whence a New Earth
Shall blossom up from.

Rosiah's eyes were golden,
Glistening orbs, absorbing,
Swooning with the slipstream,
Smitten by the palpitations
Of history so deeply drink of...

All the falsified claims,
Greed and iniquity…
They lost connection to the root,
And slandered against Yahweh.

Rosiah docked his shipped
On the banks of Lake Tana.
A multitude of men, women and children
Came to see the King of Kings…

Some from the North,
Some from the South,
Some from the East
And some from the West,
Of every hue and faith,
Of every economic strata,
Word had spread from the Rasta,
That Rosiah was coming home.

The Word for Zion

He spoke to the people thus:

"My family of all hues! My children of all branches! My joy welleth over, like a cup of wine overflowing, for a dream is now beginning in flesh. Our journey has been diverse, long and arduous through the landscapes, across oceans and over mountains, through forests and in deserts.

Unfortunately, many have lost sight of the root in a mad scramble for wealth and technological sophistication. Materiality became reality to them. Their blindness turned into a greed, like a virus in a body, but Zion shall bring healing, justice and truth!

Bring of me your tired, your weary ones wandering, looking for love, for camaraderie and sustenance. Bring me your orphans abandoned, stranded as strangers in strange lands empty handed. Bring your sick and ailing to the shores of this salve. It shall settle deeply into their wounds.

Bring your lost ones angered. Here they have a home. Bring me those oppressed by oppressors. Here they have a voice. Bring me your dreamers with eyes wanton for truth! Bring me the captains and protectors of the righteous! Let me look upon the lovers of wisdom and smile.

From this deepest root of Wisdom, we shall build a paradigm impenetrable, for Yahweh has christened...Yahweh is our bastion!

Wisdom shall reign in the classrooms and corridors wafting into streets and out into the vineyards and orchards with whistling flute from the Owl...

Healing and compassion shall echo all hospitals, for healers of Yahweh will be stationed in the medicine which draws from the infinite wells of honey balm.

Government shall be just and righteous as by starlight, not the spectacle of Babylon at odds and pitted against...

Business shall be equitable and fruitful as fields of choice wheat and plump figs from the harvest.

Wisdom will live upon Earth as it has always sought, but hitherto has been unable to abide. Let us provide a home for Wisdom...Let us prepare a home for Yahweh!

To all the Earth guidance shall be given and children will come up with the teachings of truth. The eyes of mankind will be cleansed, and no longer difference, but sameness will be understood...And the fruits of each man and woman encouraged to flourish.

Let us go back to the Garden of Eden, and listen to the *Ancient of Days*, *Elohim*, of the Ancient Wisdom which formed the Universe with Love.

Let us remember the love of Yahweh...and seek to do the will of thy plan, to carry forth love and harmony in the land, while we eat of the fruit, of the fields of thy bounty. Yah lives!

We are one forevermore. Praise the Living One...Yahweh the Redeemer!"

20 years ensued…

V. THE HOUSE OF DAVID

Upon the Throne of Zion

Rosiah Rose Rephaiah was clad in purple silk,
Black and gold satin sheets draped his throne.
The smell of frankincense rose through halls of granite stone.
The Kingdom come…
Justice will be done.

The people would often gather to hear Rosiah sing.
His heart sung of Yahweh's oneness.
The land of Zion sung.
Every word was precious silk.

The juice of peach under acacia's bloom,
The juice sopping ripe in his cup…

Peace was deep throughout the land,
Every person paid respects to Yahweh.
Love was the vibration.
Greetings of peace were melodious.
Harmony and kindness…
One loving family.

Flutes lined the royal court
Playing ancient hymns to honor sacredness.
Maidens fresh of dew lined his throne.
His daughters lovely,
Taught the teaching of love.
Not a lamb could cry without Yahweh's knowledge.

Rosiah's sons awoke to his teaching,
Acquainted daily with the grace of truth.
Rosiah watched them closely, knowing…
They shall be pure princes.
They shall love the people deeply…

Who deserves to sit atop as vice-regent of Zion?
Only the Purest.
Only the Truest.

Yahweh sees the unseen.

Now Zion was blossoming a beautiful fragrance.
The faithful came to see it.
The truthful came to praise it.
The righteous came to dwell.

It is Yahweh that redeemeth.
It is Yahweh that reviveth.
It is Yahweh that provideth.
It is Yahweh that has taught through trial.

It is Yahweh that freed us.
It is Yahweh to believe in.
It is Yahweh that enlivens.
It is Yahweh that heals.

The people live in peace. *Selah*
The people live in truth. *Shalom*

From Europe to Asia,
To the Middle East and South America,
North America had enclaves,
And Africa was Risen.

Zion exists independent of nations,
Independent of tribes,
Independent of races.
Zion is under Yahweh,
And Yahweh presides over the Universe with Justice.

Rosiah sat upon his throne in meditation...

The journey through Babylon,
The years of hardship,
The times at which only his faith
Had guided him through the night.
Only truth was sufficient for life,
And only truth could guide Zion forth.

He could not allow any compromise to justice.
He could not get lost in indulgence,
And forget the mission.
He could not allow himself wayward in luxury,
And renege on his covenant with Yah.

Rosiah rose and his eyes lit with flame.
He looked out over Zion,
Embedded in Eden,
And called his closest adviser
To make preparations,
For Rosiah was set to speak to the world.

The Word Against Israel

He spoke to the world thus:

"Your iniquities have been great. Your arrogance has been enduring.
Thereby, truth shall scald you and melt off all your leaven, to restore
Israel to its ancient Davidic splendor! And the name of Yahweh shall be
lifted high, not hidden and denied its pronunciation! This is the word of
Yahweh!

You so-called Zionists derived your right to Israel through the Tanakh,
yet few are the faithful in your ranks. You've established a nation in
union with The Beast. You will be destroyed just the same!

Oh Ashkenazi! Though our human family is one tree, you've claimed
the Jews are your genes. Now, the very Jews which resemble the
ancients face discrimination!

Recall of ancient Israel, of its ancient Davidic kingship…do you think it
would resemble your current inclinations? From dearth unto verdance,
lies into honesty, falsehood into faith, and ignorance into knowledge.
The true Zion is rising!

You've only deceived the West because the West is deceived of
themselves. For many Christian churches have distorted Yahoshua and
wield scriptures, attempting to control truth and usurp the whole

Hebraic tradition. You are in league together in a plot. You both shall fall to pieces.

My heart goes out to you! My arms are wide open! Your suffering was great in your journey through Europe, yet have fled from persecution instituting oppression…carrying discriminatory notions to Palestinian peoples, and even Mizrahi and Ethiopian Jews. If you would have encountered the ancient Israelites face to face, would you have oppressed them too?

By what right do you hold this land? For Jerusalem means City of Peace, yet it remains embroiled and divided.

You blaspheme to call yourselves Zionists. For this should be a nation under Yahweh!

Israel shall belong to the faithful. *Know this*…Zion need not this land to prosper, but Zion will overtake you and clear the land of the false. By the will of Yahweh, your ruse shall be shattered."

Vision of the Prophets

That night Rosiah dreamt of a journey to Jerusalem,
Transported on the wings of angels…

Rosiah arrived at Mount Moriah and ascended 7 levels.
When he reached the 7th level
He looked and saw a room of crystal walls.
It held 7 chairs, of ancient oak, with golden inlay,
Encircling a round table of ancient oak:
Deep mahogany, with inlaid ivory.

Rosiah stood and gazed at 6 prophets…
Amazed, he stood there enraptured.
Their cloaks were pure silk of golden thread.
Only Enoch…his face could not be seen…
The other five were anointed with a golden glaze.
The room rose with the scent of myrrh and cinnamon.

Rosiah invited them to sit and poured out water in crystal glasses.
The water was pure, so pure it glowed silver.

Enoch stood up and removed a golden flask from his cloak…
He stood over Rosiah
And blessed him silently,
Then poured a golden oil atop Rosiah's head.

Rosiah's heart swelled with a rhapsody.
He embraced their hands and wept…
His fulfillment reaching deeper rivers.

The spirit of Yahweh flooded the room,
Like a melody, a scent, a mellifluous mead,
A rain of pure raiment washing the room with velvet,
Like the taste of The Fruit of Persea.
The joy was a joy that remains.

Awakening to Blessing and Purpose

Rosiah awoke with the golden sun rising,
Shining through the lattice into his room.
His Queen, Ziza, next to him sleeping.

Rosiah rose and went to gaze over Zion,
With the knowledge
That The Third Temple must be built on Mount Moriah,
And The House of David
Must be reestablished in Jerusalem.

Dissension, Doubt and Slander

There were many around the Earth
Who loved Rosiah more.
He had been a dayspring of light in the deep night of oppression,
A firm hand to help them up,
A warm wisdom in the cold desolation of despair…

But there were those who feared Rosiah,
For he threatened their foundation.
They did not understand his love and zeal.
They doubted his wisdom, mocking Yahweh.
They slandered his name with fabricated stories.

They sought to tear down the beauty of his bastion.
They only succeeded in harming themselves.

Babylon wanted Rosiah dead,
For Rosiah rose with the underground higher.
Babylon wanted to keep the underside, deep under…

But it was destined for the underground to rise above lies.
It was destined for Rosiah to stand atop Zion,
Championing the cause of the abandoned and orphaned,
Championing the cause of the exploited workman,
Championing the cause of those facing oppression,
Championing the cause of the poor and beleaguered,

Advocating the arts of the musicians, artists and poets,
Empowering the craftsmen of various trades,
Advocating rootedness for the sake of realization,
Bringing a deep awareness of our duty to Mother Earth.

Zion brought the Truth of Balance,
While Babylon kept clambering for continuing excess.

Zion washed the flaws of the historical record clean,
While Babylon kept droning a mythos corrupt.

Rosiah was a devout servant to Yahweh the mighty.
Rosiah was vice-regent of Zion.

But there were those who wanted to plunder,
Who wanted to eat of the spoil,
Whose eyes were always wanton
For the pleasures of power,
For the pleasures of luxury,
For the pleasures of the world.

They were envious of The House of David.
They tested its integrity at every turn.
They sought to throw stones and hurl upon bricks.

Babylon smiled and feigned, inviting him to dinners,
Seeking to entangle him in ruses.

The media spun stories to smear and tarnish intention.
Rosiah watched with eyes like an owl
As they meandered and spun themselves weary.

They were a dying regime,
Desperate for an extension, to avoid their abode in the flame.

Zion stood with open arms to all people,
Awaiting their return unto life.

In prostration to Yahweh:

The Most Gracious,
The All-Knowing,
The All-Seeing,
The Almighty, Everlasting...
The All-Encompassing,
The Great Radiance of Ages,
The Most Bounteous One.
The Impregnable Bastion.
Imperishable, Imperturbable, Untarnishable Truth.

Rosiah's eyes peered past all the dissension, doubt and slander.
He looked past the rivers and mountains,
Past the stars and galaxies,
Past the kingdoms of past
And the kingdoms to come,
Past the dreams of the dreamers,
And the ether of eons,
He looked into Yahweh's eye once again.
And prostrated for guidance upon the mission at hand.
Rosiah was one with the Universe.

Transcendental Conch Shell

As Rosiah stood on his palace balcony
He pulled out a conch shell he had received as a gift
And sounded a transcendental blast.

Oracles from all over the Earth
Caught visions and premonitions,

Through the day and the night.

Within days, ten of The Righteous
Showed up at Rosiah's palace...

Rosiah and The Righteous drunk of Ademoni:
Drinks which were deep red from crushed cherries,
Pomegranates, cranberries and blackberries,
Raspberries and beets...but non-alcoholic.

The Holy Spirit filled Rosiah's palace with joy.
Rosiah's sons, daughters and wife relished the levity.
It felt like a heavenly abode.

Rosiah told them of The Vision of the Prophets
Where he ascended 7 levels and met with his fathers.

Rosiah told The Righteous to prepare for a pilgrimage.
They were going to travel to Jerusalem.

Leaving for Mount Moriah

A week passed in preparation for the journey.
Provisions were saddled on camel after camel,
Silver and gold were bagged in satchel after satchel.
Gifts the Kingdom of Zion had received
Were now gifts for the people as they'd pass.

Rosiah kissed his sons and daughters goodbye
And prayed for good graces.
He looked in Ziza's eyes and fell still...
She swelled with a beauty even greater than her constant.
Rosiah felt a joy as he knew she was pregnant,
And Ziza smiled in acknowledgement of the knowledge.
Rosiah kissed Ziza with the love of rosehips.

A festival spilled through streets
As Rosiah and The Righteous
Made their way through the crowds
Of people in celebration.

Sweet potato wafted and Ademoni flowed.
Children played peacefully over the adder's den.
The wolf nestled up and fell asleep with the lamb.

Rosiah tossed golden and silver bars to the people.
There was neither shoving, nor pulling,
Nor wrestling to obtain it. *Selah*

Northbound

Rosiah and his retinue rode into the wilderness
Down the ancient mountains northbound.

All along the way there were cheers from the people.
Rosiah threw silver and gold to them too.

At night Rosiah and The Righteous camped beneath stars.
They ate dates and recounted the biblical prophets.

Their hearts were an ocean,
Their minds were the sky,
Their bodies were the Earth,
Their breath was the ethers,
And their caravan was swaddled
By Yahweh's affection.

Their caravan climbed through the wilderness
In between towns,
Finding water sources humbly
And moving with swiftness.

They came to Port Sudan...
There they gazed upon the water,
Fresca blue and green.
The African Sun
Thick and unrelenting.

The Righteous urged Rosiah to continue North
As he looked over the water...

Rosiah reflected on the journey...

He looked upon the camels
Burdened by the weight
Of the provisions, gold and silver.
They would not make it.

He looked into the eyes of The Righteous,
And they stood for a while enmeshed.

Rosiah spoke thus:

"We must give to this town
All that we have.
Assemble the people immediately."

And that night there was a great celebration.
Ademoni flowed,
The people were gifted bars of gold and silver,
And Rosiah spoke of the beauty of Yahweh.
The people listened and ate fresh fish and vegetables.

The Wilderness

Early next morning before the town had arisen
Rosiah and The Righteous took off on caravan.
With no provisions,
Neither gold nor silver,
Just water in flasks.

They travelled with a faith of what is to come.

Days later, Rosiah and The Righteous
Had not eaten since they left Port Sudan.
They began to weaken and took repose in their tents.
Deep in the desert…
They began to pray to Yahweh.

That very day…
Manna came blowing from the sky.

They assembled the dust like the Israelites before them,
And baked cakes of Manna which tasted like cream.

All along the way they collected Manna from the sky.

The Flower of Tales

One day, many weeks into the journey,
Rosiah and The Righteous came upon a blooming flower,
It was a deep resinous blue…

At first they could not believe that such a flower
Was blooming in the desert…

They went towards it in awe
And saw it respond to their presence.
It opened its petals fuller, wider,
And it shook in the windless air.

Rosiah dismounted his camel
And took to his knees before the flower.
He smelt of its flesh,
It was fresh like warm butter.

Suddenly the flower folded inward
And began to pull back into its roots.

Rosiah put his hand in the sand,
And clasped the root before it could disappear…
It was shimmering like Lazuli.

Rosiah took out his knife
And cut the root equally amongst The Righteous.

They looked into each other's eyes with wonderment,
And ate of the mystery.

Therein, they were all transported to Mount Moriah,
Where Abraham was told to sacrifice his son.
They watched as Abraham picked up his knife to slay him,
But withheld it by Yahweh's command…

Then they were transported forward in time,

But remained in the same location...
It was an ancient threshing floor.
There was a man threshing wheat on the floor.
It was Ornan the Jebusite.

Upon the same location, but forward in time,
They appeared at the consummation of Solomon's Temple
And gazed upon Solomon and the multitudes before him
As he delivered a blessing before Ancient Israel.
Rosiah and The Righteous had tears in their eyes.

After that, they were shown the destruction of The First Temple,
By Babylonian invaders,
And the wailing, and the crying, and the fires that raged.

Next, the vision brought forth Zerubbabel,
And the wave of Israelites he led out of captivity.
It showed them The Second Temple in its beginnings and completion.

Whereby, a strange happening occurred...
The vision took them before the great grandson of Zerubbabel.
His name was Rephaiah.

Rosiah looked at him face to face and saw his own soul.
The vision showed Rephaiah in the Temple of Yahweh
Holding his young son Arnan.

Rosiah and The Righteous watched in amazement...

Then they were transported to the expansion of The Second Temple,
Followed by its destruction, by the Roman legions of Titus.

Finally, they were transported to modern times, in the near future,
And saw in its finished construction...The Third Temple.
They walked through the halls of gold and silver, with choice stone.
They stood in the inner sanctum, overcome with arching awe.

Outside, Rosiah and The Righteous looked upon a sea of people
In celebration of its construction.
People of all persuasions, of all nationalities and races,
Of every religious affiliation, in congregation before it.

It was located in the same place as the two temples before it,
On Mount Moriah,
Upon the threshing floor of Ornan the Jebusite…

That night Rosiah and The Righteous stayed up until sunrise
Telling tales of Kings, gleaning the lessons of history,
Weaving tales untold of Kingdoms like songs,
They ate Manna and drunk of a purified well…
Their hearts swelled with appreciation
For the lives which they were gifted.

Approaching Israel

Destiny was dawning her eternal dawn.
Every movement, every word seemed crafted by the master craftsman.
It seemed tailored like the sweep of eons into silver suns.
Every atom with the tender touch of Yahweh the provider.
Every pain and troubling trial was a grooming and a nurturance.
Every breath was a blessing.
Every moment was momentous.

Rosiah and The Righteous were bound by a covenant of ages,
Tightly knit like finest fabrics.
Purified like smelted silver,
Tested, tried and tested more.
Yahweh bestowed his graces in showers,
The beauty of the struggle stunning.
Ascendancy amongst men is not,
But favor under Yahweh's knowledge is.

Gold and silver store in vaults,
Could never equal Yahweh's word.
Wisdom precious silver solstice,
Golden hearts and shimmering chords.
Lined with every ruby richer,
Deeper trances dipping words,
Spreading branches, feeding roots…

Love of like a pillar risen,

Love of like a million suns,
Love of like a mission christened,
Crystal clear and shown fruition…

Rosiah and The Righteous approached the fences
Of Israel enclosed…

Through the Fences

Rosiah and The Righteous stood hundreds of meters
In front of the high tech Israeli fences
Imposed to keep out African refugees
And Islamic opponents.

Rosiah and The Righteous let go of all their camels,
And proceeded on foot without hesitation.

They came up to the fence
And all of them placed their hands upon it.
Now that Africa was risen…
Migrants from Africa seeking asylum
Was all but nil…

But in the spirit of those migrants
Who did seek asylum in the past,
And to pay homage to their struggle,
Rosiah and The Righteous scaled the fence,
Slashing their hands and arms as they scaled it…

Remember when David evaded Saul and went to Adullam?
He opened his arms to all who were in distress,
And they became strong.

Rosiah and The Righteous moved swift after scaling,
And found trenches to travel in moving Northbound.
They headed through the heat of the Negev.

The Negev

At night Rosiah and The Righteous
Took solace beneath the stars.
Yahweh provided a Well of Living Water,
And Manna from heaven for replenishment.

When Rosiah fell asleep,
Yahweh came to him in vision,
Telling him to awaken
And pick of the Myrrh tree
Down the hill where they camped.

He picked of it and awoke The Righteous.
Then in the embers of the fire
He threw in the Myrrh.
The scent was voluminous
And a spacious cloud rose…

The fire died down and everything went black.
Whereby, the flame ignited and rose.

Yahweh appeared to them
In the radiance of a thousand suns!
They recoiled, afraid that they would be destroyed.

A voice said…

"Rise…Rise and be strong."

And they felt strong.
Their eyes adjusted,
But Yahweh's face was still too luminous to be seen.
His feet were like mighty pillars,
And his arms were like mountains,
His body was like the magma of supernovas churning.

Rosiah and The Righteous began to be lifted up higher
And a verse of pure Hebrew came straight into their minds.

I have chosen you hence,

Thereby and before.
When the Universe was nonexistent,
I knew of all ending.
Fear not, but keep steady in my covenant,
And I shall bless Zion
With holiest of oils.

Jerusalem

When Rosiah and The Righteous were seen approaching Jerusalem
The IDF formed a blockade.
The people gathered in crowds.

Rosiah and The Righteous stood before them
And watched the sea begin to rock…

The Prime Minister was called and brought forth.
Rosiah stepped forward to meet him.

He spoke to the prime minister thus:

"Let us pass, by the will of Yahweh
We have come.
For the sake of truth
We have labored.
For the love of peace
We continue.
And for the people of this planet,
We shall embrace.
All our welcome in our kingdom,
Zion is for the balance,
To smite the Beast."

Rosiah's eyes were swollen, pregnant with wisdom,
Compassionate and calm…
The Prime Minister softened.
By The Great Spirit of Truth, he was disarmed.

By Yahweh's will not a man could contend,
Not a nation could defy without ramification.

The people felt the glow of Rosiah and The Righteous.
They followed them through the streets
Towards Mount Moriah.

The sky became orange.
The wind smelled of myrrh.
Children stopped playing and began to meditate.
Birds stopped singing and were soothed.
Palestinians and Israelis brought down their guards.
A pulse radiated through the Earth.

Family members which had been fighting
Called one another.
Things which were long forgotten
Were recalled.

Love began to rise on the waters...
Planes equipped with bombs
On missions to deploy,
Diverted and refrained
From attacking their targets.

Hearts opened and the rivers of consciousness were cleansed...
Everlasting peace and virtue began to reign.

Rosiah and The Righteous approached Mount Moriah.

A Premonition

It had been 9 months since the caravan took off,
And Rosiah felt a deep stirring within.
He walked up to a passerby
And reached out his hand...
The passerby, entranced,
Handed over his phone.

Rosiah called Ziza
And told her to immediately catch a flight to Jerusalem.
He called the Israeli government and told them of her coming.
Rosiah's son would be born very soon.

The Threshing Floor

Rosiah and The Righteous
Made their way up through streets.
They felt a pulsation,
A pulling, a glowing sensation,
A feverish pull began to take hold of Rosiah.

He began to run towards this feeling…
He sprinted with the spirit of deliverance.
It was the threshing floor of Ornan the Jebusite…
The Foundation Stone
Under the Dome of the Rock.

Coming to the Dome
Rosiah began to go into a trance.
He walked on The Temple Mount
As if in a dream…

Walking into the Dome
He fell into the deepness.
Stepping over the railing
He knelt on the hallowed ground,
Thousands of years away…
All the chaff of millennia was being winnowed away.

Rosiah spoke thus as he kneeled:

"This is my home,
I've come home to Judah,
To the site of the temple I've known.
Praise Yah…

My son shall not live in Babylon's babble,
As I have had to wander many years through its rattle.
But Judah shall be his abode…"

The Righteous were in awe as they listened,
Watching Rosiah kneeling on The Foundation Stone.

Rosiah took a deep breath and looked up,

Then told three of The Righteous
To get Ziza from the airport…

The Birth of Arnan

When Ziza arrived
She was breathing with labor.
The Righteous laid pillows and cloth on the threshing floor.
Then Rosiah asked for everyone to wait outside.
Only he and Ziza were left in the Dome.

On The Foundation Stone, Ziza gave birth…
Rosiah assisted with tender concern.

It was a swift birth,
And Ziza was graceful.
Her smile was the light of Zion realized.
She held her son close and kissed him.

Rosiah kissed Ziza, hugging her,
Swaddling his wife and son in his arms.

He stood up, then picked up his son,
Looking in his eyes…
They glistened like orbs of black wellspring,
Twinkling inklings of otherness…
A triangle of raised flesh was on his forehead.

Rosiah held him and said…
"Arnan…Arnan my son."

Joy filled his heart,
A blooming joy,
A crying jubilant joy!!!
Rosiah Rose Rephaiah,
Father of Arnan.

In **1 Chronicles 3:21** in The House of David,
Rephaiah is father of Arnan.

In Hebrew, Rephaiah means 'Yahweh is healing.'
Arnan means 'Joyous Shout.'

VI. THE THIRD TEMPLE

In the Interim

And 77 weeks hence...
The Earth had overturned.
The seas had come into a cleansing.
The forests at encroachment from dozers,
Began growing.

The foundation stone glowing,
Showing a fountain of force from the Ultimate Ocean...

Rosiah convened with imams, priests and rabbis,
Preachers, ministers, monks and holy men.
Sages and architects,
Governors and presidents,
Foreign dignitaries and entrepreneurs...

Artists and activists,
Artisans and craftsmen,
Musicians and dreamers,
Farmers and fishermen,

Journalists and gentlemen from all sectors of society,
Women from all fields and areas of work.

Rosiah met with the youth
In the cities, and the countryside.

He visited the vineyards,
The groves and fruit orchards.

He found solace under a tamarisk tree in Beersheba,
And stood on the banks of Galilee and sung grace.

In Palestine, Rosiah was greeted with a chanting.
In Jerusalem he established his abode.

Unto all the Earth Rosiah's arrival resounded,
His love for Yahweh the Supreme overflowed.

The Temple Vision

Unto the night in Jerusalem,
The soft strumming lyre put him 'sleep,
As Ziza stroked his head...

The Golden Helix was revealed, and unfolded,
And a mirror image cast a shadow of its shimmering,
A drop of golden seed dripped from its edges,
It settled on The Temple Mount as a glowing semicircle.

It was white marble with gold veins,
And its doors opened before him.

A golden light like excelsior
Exceeded his pupil,
But a voice called forth with instruction...

"Community floweth through these chambers,
And dreams coalesce in this symbol."

Zeh Kathuv...it was engraved on the seal of the entrance.
Zeh Kathuv...it was written in stone.

Assembling the Details

Rosiah awoke with a fervent pulsation.
He awoke with a blueprint
For the temple's creation.

He called up the craftsmen,
The artists and sculptors,
The hewers of stone
And carvers of wood.
He called up the architects and told them his vision.

They convened at his home in Jerusalem,
In his meeting room secluded.
They worked from morning unto next morning,
Drinking Ademoni

And eating sweet potatoes,
Hemp seed and olive oil.

They fleshed out the blueprint,
Hammered home details,
And called up providers
For raw source material.

Logistics were fixed
And things set in motion.
24 hours had passed...
The basic plan had emerged.

Rosiah called for a pronouncement
Upon Mount Moriah,
Outside of the Dome of the Rock.

The Word of the Temple

2 days hence...

Rosiah stood in the company of The Righteous,
In the company of an imam, Christian priest and rabbi.

There were thousands gathered to hear the pronouncement.

Rosiah spoke to them thus:

"There is One, and only One.
One Root and One Drum.
One People, One Earth...One Universe.
Yahweh is One.

From the seed,
Earth sprung.
From the clay
And wet soil...
Yahweh blew breath
Into the nostrils of Adam.

Seven generations went by...

Enoch walked with Yah.
Enoch in Hebrew denoting 'dedication.'
Enoch symbolizes an example of devotion.

The religion of Enoch
Existed before David,
Before Israel and Abraham…

Before the Quran,
New Testament and Tanakh,

Before the branchings of Abrahamic traditions,
Before the branchings of mankind.

No Israelites, no Ishmaelites,
No separate clans of which to speak,
Just the pristine faith
Of Enoch the prophet.

As the Universe hath sprung from One Root…
Yahweh.
All life comes from One Root.

Mankind comes from One Root, of Adam.
And the faith of Enoch is the glistening vine,
The True Vine.

It is the true twine in The Root of David,
The root of the lineage that unfolded.

In this…Muslim, Christian and Jew can unite.
In this True Vine humanity coalesces."

And that day the Dome of the Rock was demolished,
And the building of The Third Temple commenced.

…And the Nebula split open.
The egg cracked in half.
The original faith,

The original origination…

That night Enoch came to Rosiah in vision.

The Vision of Enoch

Enoch approached Rosiah
And took off his hood.
He looked in his eyes
And a tear fell from his cheek.

He spoke with a heavy tongue,
Of an Ancient Melody,
While he smiled at Rosiah tenderly…

"Well done.
Well done Rephaiah.
You are the Fruitful Bough…
The unfolding lotus fragrance.

You shall bear the blessings of Joseph
And wield the scepter of Judah.
Peace be upon you and Ziza forever.
Amen."

The Third Temple Erected

Unto 77 weeks passed another,
And there were all the people gathered…
Like in the vision,
From *The Flower of Tales*.

And there the temple stood,
Just like in the vision.

Rosiah and The Righteous
Walked through the halls of gold and silver, with choice stone.
In the inner sanctum they stood and gathered hands.
They prayed unto Yahweh the Gracious…

Streams and plumes of smoke perfumed outward,

Sending out incense,
A fragrance of frankincense
Wafting through the streets.
Yahweh's great grace manifest in the vapors.

As they prayed
The sun reached its zenith,
The moon bore burdened a full eclipse,
And the Earth stopped to meditate
On the meaning of Yahweh.

Rosiah and The Righteous emerged with the sun,
Glistening health, vitality and love,
Vibrating forgiveness, acceptance and patience.

They raised their fists in joy
As the people cheered in celebration.

Rosiah and The Righteous
Looked upon the thousands.
Their hearts swelled with love.
Their eyes were red like wine with a love...
Of a Love Supreme,
Of a dream become flesh,
And the flesh of one body,
As humanity come to Oneness.

Rosiah spoke to the people thus:

"And unto every avenue traversed,
All tributaries flow unto One.

From the root it has risen!
By a well of living water.

By the will of El Elyon
The tree of life sprung."

A Mission Completed

A week later, in The Third Temple
Rosiah Rose Rephaiah stood in the inner sanctum
Holding his young son Arnan.

He spoke to Arnan thus:

"Arnan...turn your heart unto Yahweh like Enoch.
Turn your whole soul unto Yah's Golden Light.
Drinketh from the Everliving Well and find peace.

Walk in the Ancient Ways
That never find blemish.

Root yourself in The Root
And give praise to Yahweh."

THE END

Information About the Author:

Johnathan Abraham Antelept is the Founder, Owner and CEO of STONE OF XAVIER LLC.

Contact Information:

johnathan.antelept@stoneofxavier.com

CPSIA information can be obtained
at www.ICGtesting.com
Printed in the USA
JSHW021221250222
23320JS00001B/39

9 781732 600911